New Fields and Other Stones

On A Child's Death

New Fields
and
Other Stones

On A Child's Death

Poems

Saul Bennett

Archer Books

These poems first appeared in the following publications:
"Hot Dog," *Amelia*, #26, 1998
"Measurements," *The Christian Century*, Feb 7-14, 1996
"Bagged," *The Christian Century*, July 30-August 6, 1997
"A Wake Night," *ELF: Eclectic Literary Forum*, Spring 1997
"Jesus Matinees," *First Things*, May 1996
"Resuscitation," *Pudding Magazine*, #35, 1997

Portions of this book have been excerpted in the limited edition chapbook, *Jesus Matinees and Other Poems*, Pudding House Publications, 1998

Jacket cover photo © 1998 by John Tribulato

Printed and manufactured in the United States of America by Archer Books

First Edition

Library of Congress Catalog Card Number: 98-070021

ISBN 0-9662299-0-8

Archer Books
Post Office Box 1254
Santa Maria, CA 93456-1254

http://www.archer-books.com

For Joan, Sara, Charles, Lizzy

Contents

New Fields and Other Stones

Enrolled in first born's first
night suckle
workshop, straying caterpillar

fingers sanding angel
fluff on gently angled
scalp, my wife arrives

upon a prospect she never
said she was sure
she wished to settle.

I

PAY PHONE

Grieving you float manacled
to the Penn Station
pay phone

that morning you used
to reach upstate Emergency
physician awaiting

death train home
to begin the mad
ride there.

How could you know your wife
from home on the line
with him

when your call cut
through told him *Don't
tell him. He'll collapse.*

*I'll tell him when
his train gets here.*
Your child.

PINING

Seeing sticking out of the heads of the open coffins gigantic
price tags
he screamed. Guilty,

As his living parts preferred to buy low for the launch
two days hence
one flight up

In their chapel, in keeping with his faith's ancient design on dust
to dust plainest pine
he dropped his head

Over the heart of a mid-priced stained and finished number so his
daughter's spirit wouldn't
mark him cheap.

LONG PANTS RELAY TEAM

So she shouldn't for a moment
be alone
before the funeral
someone said go
hire the Orthodox to sit
saying prayers before
her coffin
in the parlor where
they brought her today after
yesterday's

sudden death.
Till Sunday they sat
in succession bobbing below
black half moon beaver
hats transporting, each
for hours in silence, to dampened
lips the issue of slender
books in Hebrew. I shook
the hand of the last, younger,
even, than our daughter.

AN UNDERTAKER RECOUNTS HIS YOUTH

A good *thousand* I tell you he buried
by 21.

In the newsroom others called him
Death

For his suppleness and poise under
heartbreak

Of the bereaved dangled at the end
of his line

Left hanging no more miserably at the end
than when

He began to probe, sigh, wheedle, sigh, cadging
a next day's

Obituary from a next-of-kin. Interviewing
himself

Now for tomorrow's paper he fails
to soothe

Searching for the plot of his daughter's
life.

THE NEWS OF THE WORLD

I

In "morgues," newspapers lodge in drawers eternally,
as of some remains remain in morgues transitionally,
file fotos of the gone and here, for publication

Upon exhumation, sowing reward or punishment of resurrection,
at the discretion of editors thwacked by lower
back pain, breaking news, whimsy, vodka; groused

To fiddling with file fotos face figures' fate forever,
or just for today; anointing today, say, a mustache
phenomenally philanthropic, two academically gifted,

One supernaturally wise, she from society ostracized,
several reportedly victimized, the allegedly heroic
and supremely athletic, the freshly coupled, an uncouple

Caught coupling, those roundly esteemed, likewise erotic, the more
than marginally plain for a day; morgues billeting, as well, many
of their own, ponder now this picture, luckless product of my flesh.

II

Smiling file foto face,
smile suspended
scaled suiting

story seams surrounding
one-half column
pix beneath

Paper's
writer dies
at age 24

Rejiggering time, rejecting
piton, rope, fear, smile
ascending years only

faith can map, appeasing
needs of climbers tomorrow;
smile smiling through

cushioned condolences conveyed
by those distant; divining
copped dreams of ones

decimated; smile immune
at machine copy edges to slowly
burning crust of projecting years.

Yet in my faith's tradition
I renounce as expedient
but messianic a fotocopy smile;

for while sniffing the absence
of embalmment's sugars I feel
its oils chill, watch them blanche

file foto smile. I embrace,
instead, value-added
pain procurable only

from file foto smile lashed
to original newsprint; smile
to tan toward a movie sepia,

warming, moderately tropical
in tone, with dawn potential.
In two dozen years or a

million, time darkened
newsprint file foto smile grows,
dims, whispers, withers, trembles,

chips, shatters on approach
or threat of touch, flecks
freed, romping now over blankets

spilled across time's
disorderly cradle, tiny toes
teased then over first

fire, awaiting summons
with sisters for reformation
into baby's first shoe bronzed.

A JOURNALIST'S REPORT
FROM THE FRONT

Thwarted by the absence of a fixed
    aesthetic
As to how she looked at the virtual
    moment of death,
I have only her supervisor's description
    to paint on.
Like her, a journalist, he outlined deliberately
    a portrait
in cold true type—wait!

They use offset printing now, or computer
    doodads:
Pack in that old Linotype imagery. And it isn't
    cold,
Whatever they use. If I could get it fixed
    true
In my picture brain, locking it in that
    contrary
View finder until my building binding pain
    squeezes
The trigger, I could die the life mere
    vanity
Or worthless softness bars me now from departing.

You might possibly finally agree. Not that you
    would want to watch
Your daughter die. But on entering this theatre
    at any hour
Of a summer's night, were you I, how long would you wait
    for the picture to begin?

TERMINUS

Did the baby cream
and bunting blue
and chick maize

Tile chips that grant
mosaic life
to letters

Grand Central

Grieve and run
wet at once
to cleanse

Knowing

The day
my daughter
died

Owing

Me for as a boy
I often scaled
this platform rock

To see
my aunt at 91
alive still in the Bronx?

THE COMMUTER

As one killed my child
I know brain
aneurysms liquidate

at 24.
But on my
train this evening

stands this woman
from our town, her
airless face a pummeled

paper sack. "Aneurysm
survivor. Rare! Rare! A good
70, don't she

look? Ya know, she's
50?" whispers he
who points her out

with a discoverer's
pride two months after
my baby died, blabbing all

I hated to hear
how this creature
with the lucky leak

lived. Now wanting terribly
to resent her every tick
tock, I find

I am unable. On
my insides instead
I give her a kiss.

PAUL REVERE IN MOURNING

On the "T" my wife and son a row behind
my daughter bore my hand and sentry watched
me cry discreetly rolling toward the North End
for Italian with no reservation on my birthday past
her sister's hundred days' precisely unexpected
death Her mother's high

          sigh

          at every

          stop

          along
Tripped me When we finally sat
          the long
   The bread was good but wine
          cool
  He served in short stem glasses
          October

          Friday

          evening

          route

RESUSCITATION

Whenever without warning
her name preceding
the last of another

appears below before me
in a black daylily field
of print I press opposing

thumbs hard and flat applying
utmost pressure against
the page obliterating

all in the rigid row save
Sara thus restoring to my eye's
heart my daughter's beat

GREENS

Ridged differently, countersunk, this newest rectangle,
    its grass a nursing green, greener than grass
mothering older harder smoother neighbor rectangles,
    their forms long since more imputed than apparent.

Intaglio in feeling (cruel that word, assigned this
    topography when swayers on high crave relief),
in its January infant greenness, this one, a tiny
    transient bronze platter bearing letters only
pressing the earth at its feet, bawls at strangers
    tipping toward learned green tops fathering their own
extended boxes, and pierces hearts, or would,
    if the name on the plate could grow dates.

"Aiii! Look, a marker only this one got.
    So new yet! No stone even, would you look,"
at my darling daughter's declining mound.
    At some unknown hour, time's riposte to
grief amassed: intaglio bequeathed relief.
    God, if I'm lucky.

MEASUREMENTS

With my pocket magnifier,
just a complaisant slip
like a flattened tortoise head
lacking color,

from its narrow soft plastic
navy case, a piddling tool
that now a half-year "afterward"
has discovered—*what luck!*—

permanent lodgings
in the shabby interior
of my wallet, I explore
impulsively again

my darling daughter's
face, her eyes in Sara's
last earth-shot at 24
5 months 8 days;

Sara, her mother, sister,
I; we, looking pleased
in quickfreeze-pose
seconds before our Taps

"solongHonloveyoucall"
12 days before *suddenly*
without warning
in perfect health our first-

born is struck. This 1
by 3 silly promo freebie
across my universe
trained, unrehearsed

down, up, floating
upon its subject, she
my successor, muted, is
God's true instrument.

A NOTE ON THE RUN
FROM A BARITONE ON TOUR

Encouraged by our therapist I screamed
in the beginning in the basement
but frightened so those
upstairs I retreated inside
a speeding sealed car or better afoot on rural
weekend desolate roads feeling no inhibition burning
my throat I screamed so each time three or four long noon
factory whistle blasts then feeling guilt for not
continuing resuming
a hundred lengths later fearing
but half hoping a local would pounce
and scold or summon from miles off the trooper. Subsiding
once I wondered
quizzed
if I could whisper
more than I did it
for with no warning one morning our child.

INSTALLED

March below the snow over the phone
I went hunting for the stone
Hacking through to bone
Of my upright afterlife *alone*.

My first call to the cemetery
Raised a voice dripping Derry
(Strange, alien, on this ground). Eager,
He sounded, finding my knowledge meager.

"Who nearby can cut me a footstone?"
"Easy that, sir!" Back he came
Shoveling name after name, tone
Celibate, commensurate with this game.

Three I called, stating my needs;
Inside, doped, dreaming of weeds
And withering, cursing past "crises;"
Outside, hysterically calm, scribbling prices.

The styles each offered, it turned
Out, were identical—cemetery rules—
But the temperature of two voices burned
Me some—they lacked fire, the fools!

To sound so cool quoting costs! I thought:
Appear interested. Better: concerned!
The third, not lowest, had learned
My text of warmth, so from Mario I bought.

His mother, Jessica, I met *en route*
When I called one time addressing
Their sketch. Her *"So distressing*
For you" was decently soft but acute.

"Especially her young age." Another damn law
—*Jesus!*—says no new stones till late spring
(Earth's too hard), so in June I'll bring
Us to my daughter's grand opening (damn thaw).

II

FEATURE PRESENTATION

Sign atop, brass,
medium beneath, cinema:
cobbled, grainy preview
newsreel authenticating
yearlong excursion
through maiden regions
of malted ether.

Brass removed, stone
implanted, replacing, begins
ascending romance,

our child's sudden death
off screen, embracing
living theatre
raging with, what life?

THE GRIEFMOBILE

Our silence deepens and lengthens
discussions we avoid
on the topic of our

dead child. When at first we began
to not engage her times
and life in shifting movements

within our late
model grieving machine, idling
instead into well lighted

established safe avenues
of conversation rustled
along by a warning

breeze, I imagined our
behavior apostasy. It is
not. It is prayer.

CAPITAL

A check for 36 thousand our daughter's sudden
death birthed,
job policy proceeds. At first

I thought to use a third
to cover funeral
and plot but I could

not. Instead I swapped
with her and paid myself with
the last of my liquid

so she could be the one
who paid her sister's final
college bill. Two thirds I took

and sealed inside a distant
new account and never stole
a pound. Yesterday I closed it

out and moved
the balance in with mine.
Though not so

pressed for cash
I felt it time to bring
our child home.

REVEILLE

From grief at last paroled perhaps?
Primping smartly, I go along, but far
too con cagey to tip memory new address:

this passed on, hard worn, steamed
to a fake high shine ex's suit
time's warden fits me for, heeling me

out his coop's door, I see, is coarse
close up, misshapen, saddled with bumps,
stained in exposed shameful places, secret

seams prone to pop, need needles soon. So no,
furlough's, not parole's, the word—
these duds won't get me far. That's it,

or less: the smallest piece of peace, just
you'll see, like an old Army weekend pass,
briefest freedom. "Liberty," they called it,

but they made you return Monday reveille
or out they'd sic their sidearm waving
M.P. posses. Sure, a "shorty's" all,

I'll bet. But hold! What's so grand,
anyway, a crank parole silent, moving
picture shot to show my daughter's grieving

pa? Parole's at most that same buttoned booth,
only in eternal flight, a dream cage, with
shriveled eyes but can see stalk marks

hoofed by the projectionist: shadow lit,
immense, svelte, a Doberman, black, goose
stepping upon my own shortened currents.

For Frank Bergon

BALLOON MAN

I

Feeding at one end
I watch my daughter's words

    lofted
    toward
    friends
    across

    pause in flight

    reassemble beneath
    the chandelier bisecting
    our dining table

    regather speed
    abandoning
    original course

       bend
     in
    formation
due south

into my mouth

a silly procession

II

Six balloons
uninflated stemmed oval wafers
silver dollar size
beige
oxford grey
black

Two
each

Rank rubber
feeding forefinger forced
by some anonymous

Party at a zoo
a visitor
female
coaxing the little aviators through the tunnel entrance

I appearing a small
fur bearing animal, tamed,
one could nuzzle at home,

Balloons inflating
to full munitions strength

    baby rockets
    golf ball size
    gagging me
    of course

Some *sss*-ing flat

III

Dizzy now but working
a handy nod and concealed
idiot's grunt
I fashion clumsy *"Ex-queues"*

Push up desperately parched
grasping rubber jackets
sucking off emergency juices
from my upper palate

Rolling to starboard
discarding the deck
of table conversation
I wobble off

Tongue racked upon
        two
ripened balloons

Blown up
still
inside me

The blacks

Twin depth charges fired off
at once bearing me fleeing
        deeper below
into the claiming sea

In the bathroom mirror I bite
        hard chewing
off the unexploded words

                "When my
                sister
                died last
                year...."

ON THE RACK

A permanent pocket
of madness our heavenly bespoke
shroud maker slashes into the lining

Of my brain; a trick exploding pocket;
in public, quiescent, packed
full to bursting but flat

On the outside. Within, on no
notice, a paunchy atom splitting, infinite
entrails

Of my grief, over
my child's
grave.

FIFTH COLUMN

Our child might have died four times at least.
She aspirated on a carrot when
I picked her up at two to dance. I died
myself that time the horrid waiting in
Emergency. At eight an ocean life-
guard brought her in. Fifteen, a horse blew up
and took a bite but only left a scar.
That time a Maui waters man 'o war gave
thirty stings but mostly shock was all.

July. Bastille Day. Thursday. Morning.
Nine. She's twenty-four. Health splendid. In love.
Loved. At work she puts her hand to head:
You know? I think I have a headache. Goes
down. Like that. Stays. I'm blessed four times with what
I banked before. Say you? Yes you—spare a dime?

SWAP SHOP

I

Baited then hooked
by short line
on a poster

Left of cashier
at a takeout
CLAMS OYSTERS

Piercing my skull
with its knell
for my monster

*If it loses an eye
something else will grow
back on a lobster*

Knowing this now
I'd swap me
for low order

So early could see
with new heart
my late daughter

II

In the end the only death
was vision in one eye,

touching my sleeve
as might a mourner

she told me on the platform.
I knew her first

as a rumor, a one-of-a-kind
angel who'd licked a brain

aneurysm. When I saw her,
my age, first, she was my old

Aunt Rose. Today we were sister
and brother. At my name she went

Ahhh . . . oh! and said she'd read
in the papers of the "extra-

ordinary" life of my daughter.
When our train came she pawed air.

ON ENCOUNTERING THE FATHER
OF A DEAD CHILD AND,
SUBSEQUENTLY, THAT CHILD

I

I dread I know to say to him
the thing I heard I thought
to say that saw me through
were I to be within him then.

Not I knew that he would care
or even pay me mind behind
the mask he bought on time
from God to act him through

The worst. No matter where
I saw him then I saw him from
one side was all until he turned
so we could see our face.

II

He fled the site of his own
child,
sighting

her, say
half a block away,
engaging

another, always
before she could see
him retreating,

assuring himself
each time, atoning,
he too soon might die.

RAVEL'S *PIANO CONCERTO IN D MAJOR FOR THE LEFT HAND*

Years after his right hand was blown off in the Great War
the Austrian pianist Paul Wittgenstein
came to perform the new left hand
concerto composed
in his honor
in 1931.
This
bass
cranky
dour stump
of a piece has
been a favorite
for years, owing some
to my lefthandedness. But
since reading in a book written
by a father whose young child died
suddenly that such a loss is akin to an
amputated limb, this left tube feeding enriches
the simmering cavity accommodating my fetched legs.

For Nancy Shear

GALLOWS OBSERVED IN SUMMERTIME

Though tethered more pliably now
to the slanting poles staked
skyward at the same abrupt intervals across
the five precision hedgerows of type cast cold
against this immaculate

God silent card of snow,
approached at risk a year past their hurried
formation, these black noosy loops
strangle the scent
of my slowly seasoning grief.

The family of

Sara Bennett

acknowledges with grateful

appreciation your kind expression

of sympathy

BOX LIFE

I Inspector Virus

Over fading second beer
Under league's leading
Night, muggiest, year,

Under falling white ball
Recessed high atomic
Yellow ceiling light,

Under opaque living room
Coffee table (shape: infield,
Approximately; color: infield

Dirt, but darker; top, Formica)
A small triangular slab
Of forgotten (hah!) mourners'

Hard box seat, foot square,
Accepted 13 months before,
Napali fake mahogany cat orange

Stripe processed corrugated skin;
Exterior, falsified as my own;
Interior, as mine, sealed air

And wild pitch; tense: future
Past imagined, obtrudes slightly,
Fouling ground of healing

Shag rug fields, revealing
To slightly tipsy eye
A Javert virus, invisible,

Released from seat through
Cop's porous dagger crease
Exposed angle trouser leg,

Rejuvenating germ originated
To start my hounded year;
This stickiest mortal gumshoe,

Unroutable, deliberate,
Crossing over
Through every night;

Javert box sole survivor/hunter
Original litter of four,
Undertaker dispatched, assigned

One each survivor immediate:
Sister, brother, mother,
I; mates buried

In prickly haste in basement
Heap at tail of first mourning
Week: *shiva* ends; shiver, never.

II *Sonderkommando*

Box's gone.
Come for.
Last night.
Confiscated; removed, no aroused

Neighbors to *tsch-tsch*
Poor Jew, with garbage
But left uncoffined, exposed
At property line. Not

Any box: *shiva* box,
In ingenuous hiding, snuggled
18 months *L'Chaim!*
Beneath huge living room trap

Door top open sides peeking out
This much
Coffee crypt. An Anne
Frank, after a fashion,

Box then:
Jew female exposed,
Last remaining
Main floor remains

Of my daughter's mourning
Week. Came no Nazis
Per se, merely a Gestapo
Aneurysm. Cleaner. I'd crossed

Fingers our child's
Mother would not dis-
Cover final box, resume dis-
Belief, renounce, through me,

Oust: assign
Child's own father
To carry out
Transport to curb, consign.

Shiva—initial seven-day mourning period

Sonderkommando—Jewish prisoner on Holocaust
                       extermination camp crematoria
                       detail

For Annette Kramer

III

AFTER THE ARCHITECT

The upstairs room in the house rebuilt by angels after
    the explosion
retained left over matter scorched. For a good year
    or longer
he made do with the remains of the old furnishings
    unempowered, useless
essentially. He had a place to lie down screaming without
    a sound
and a seared mattress springs thieved. But its location kept
    shifting and often
even in daylight he stumbled and cried falling sideways landing
    —and this was odd—
on interior slate hard black earth. Then the rooms began
    to fill
slowly with furniture of increasingly radical design he did not
    choose
but could not oppose. Soon he cooked for himself. He loved a good
    egg bullseye up
or precision over easy from the old days beneath predictable
    control.
But he felt now they might kill him cooked that way so he scrambled
    with unintended
exotic ingredients, indigo cheese growing wildly in fields, fuschia
    herbs plucked from
gigantic rocks surrounding the house reaching the upstairs
    windows.
He ate with his eyes shut. The omelettes took some getting
    used to
but tasted fresh and delicious. He sought new fields and other
    stones.

THE GREY WHITE WAY

To breathe aloud at midday softly
your dead child's name now less

than two years past is to be grazed
suddenly on the forehead in a grey silent

dawn cobbled street by an immense paper
bag filled with feathers hefted by a shave

needy beggar wearing a raggedy
suit and torn wingtip shoes once he wore

to important business. His stained fedora
and yours are identical.

RENDER HOMAGE
TO KATHARINE LEE BATES (1859-1929),
AUTHOR OF THE HYMN,
AMERICA THE BEAUTIFUL

I

Yom Kipper morning attend mass
Of beer bottles
Gripping garage refrigerator shelf
Nearest heaven as faithfully

As surrounding gumshoe
Flock embraces his Holy Father
When the Vicar of Christ deigns
Depart discomforts of Rome;

Morning count: 21 escorting
Psalmists, blending 12 earnest
Local lagers, 9 choice
Imported premium ales,

Brown bottle bullet busting
Label vestments serializing
Sandwich board style
Psalms upbeat surrender.

II

Catch laughing squirrel
Tag team thumb tails at this Jew's
Inherited notion of Days of Awe
Devotion without worldly motion

Play claw gitty little globes
Across freshly overturned
September stocked earth
For 18 seconds or so—

L'Chaim!—before scratching
For the stars along backyard's
Broad bark boulevard beneath pin
Oak leaves making early autumn *Aliyah.*

III

Out of her sermon
Deck rabbi suddenly pulls
Resurrection,
An essentially Christian hole card,

Inviting browsed prayer book
Rear's raised silent bid announcing
Revelation,
Propping my nearly folded hand.

Eyes open now
I continue dozing
Across the flattish waves
Of her sermon

But reading now witness
The Dead are a return race,
This forecast on my page realized ex-
Quisitely as I part the sea of the second

Stanza of the 1893 Bates composition.
Yes of course surely she knew
My child, born 77 years after into
Their intertwined future, or why would she

Preach *O Beautiful for pilgrim feet,*
Whose stern, impassioned stress,
A thoroughfare for freedom beat,
Across the wilderness?

Circling not all at once but together
Nonetheless *The Dead are a return race,*
Forming a legion ascendant
Jogging in uniform doubletime,

Jersey bearing numbers billowing
Toward and even touching
But failing to bend
The arch withdrawing tape,

Young woman in the lead rank,
High consistent stride swelling
The entire legion's resolve to return.
The Dead are a return race

As through the open temple window
They are seen washed
In white smoke, stroking nearer
Return. At the service break

From a neighboring balcony seat
The mother who slipped me
Her pen minutes before asks
Holding her child's hand

What thing am I writing
This writing proscribed holiest day?
When I reveal this poem's
Stem her daughter seated she says

Is 6; her son would be
8 had he not at 5 months
Died. He then too is seen
Returning, bounding at the breast

Of my child dead a year
At 24 pilgrim footed hurdling the opening slowly
Gigantic white holy holly rings.
The Dead are a return race.

IV

At bedtime refrigerator
Depletions alter the score
As I close that door
Counting psalms, 18 to adore.

Aliyah—an ascension

THREE DREAMS AND OUT

I Tourists

Asleep the present
absence of my elder daughter
appears to baffle her younger
brother, sister, mother, me.

Where is Sara? we are asking,
room emptied of other life,
possessions save chairs,
although we remain standing,

Tourists wandering in a scattered
parts circle, attempting
to read from a too great distance
to see clearly bus route signs

In an African language lashed
to steel poles at a deserted
queue in a land bisecting
the equator of my soul. Waking,

My mouth is stuffed
past full by
pillow corner, informing me
before dawn Sara is dead.

II Three Hundred Seventy-Two

I awaken to my
child as myth
one year one week

past her death.
In my dream others
say she conforms

—a lie.
They taunt her.
Appearing later

to supplicate
on one knee rubbing
Eleanor's underside

I inform the July
mourning air: "See?
See? How they slander

the dead?" In freshly
cut grass sweet fumes
her purr revives me.

III   Spa Dream

In this dream so old
I go alone to Saratoga Springs.

The spa I seek I find
without a wasted step.

I knew it once before
in middle age. We went there

many times. The last we took
with us a pride of plastic bags

and all but dead and maybe still
we stuffed them with our daughter's.

OVERBOARD!

Across the stormy autumn
   phone his raging
      waves pounded so

      I sat sinking off the edge of an end berthed
      kitchen counter stool a coast away
      knuckling my tight night time scalp
      kneading news an old friend's son
      eve birthday 29 had sought as
      threatened to swallow his
      beyond only two years past
      my own loving life daughter's
      —p*oof!*—at her desk, brain, 24.

      So who was he to corner me? Waiting
      at the end of his "12-to-15" pumped
      Valium visit was a holding ward, no
                       fucking
                footstone.

           But *shhh* . . .
          knuckles,
         again all ears,
       resumed
      their dig,
     clawing deeper, pre-
    historically.

Who was I to adjudicate the impossible?

MAGELLAN'S SECRET SAILING

After she died suddenly he took
to taking long very hot
bubble baths fall and winter
weekend late afternoons

Reading each soak a back issue
or two of major Sunday paper
book reviews lifted
from his firm's library

Entertaining at first new
suitor slyly the shyest
beam of dusky tunnel light
but soon with mind's eye

Aggressiveness akin to his
business's pursuit of business
the possibility though a long way
to sale that such an ambitious

Reverse evensong navigation
of words berthing
sometimes at lasting literature
would baffle and finally

Dissipate time enabling rescue
of his young adult daughter
slipped aboard between *Children's
Bookshelf* and *Science Fiction.*

For Roslyn Marcus

ESTEEMED MAJOR POETS MEMORIALIZE
A DEAR POET FRIEND

On the ear the poems they read appear to look so—
    Protestant.
Each maker makes them want to soar you feel but in their
    measured breaths
they kite quite low. Perhaps because their friend is dead
    these poet
household names are clutching too much string. Who would care
    two years ago
but in this 60-minute Quaker pew tonight a Jew I come to mourn
    again and still
my child. I ask then why in Jesus' name they can't or won't provide
    for meal
the thunder owed to meet my daughter's need. Of course they don't
    know who she was
or who I am. But must they let irrelevant detail deprive their kites
    of higher sail?

JUST DESSERT

"For your dessert—disfavor rummed with death?"
the Captain speaks, our menus blanked of sweets
shown others having left again he greets
not mordantly. *"That's* the lot? Save your breath
and produce this *du jour,"* I snap beneath
his virgin pad, surrounding finger beats
in maddened time survivors' angry bleats.
"I trust you'll crust dessert with frosted wreath?"

The hollow cast that staged dessert had dressed
in shrouds before though horizontally.
My mother's father's brother, Holocaust—
he led. Behind, my wife's great aunt caressed
my father's son. At curtain gradually
the Captain bowed, announced our daughter, lost.

BAGGED

Cerebral palsy came today to take
our daughter's clothes. Two years it took to call
then go below alone last night to rouse
the condemned cartons, heavy each a soul,
and bid them join the prostrate bags my wife

had filled by day. I helped the driver load
the sprawling sacks into the bursting back-
side of the seething August truck. Before
I knew I threw one unencumbered by
whose flesh in flight then smothered my contempt.

A DURABLE POWER

His death papers in the mail
my uncle 83 sends me 500 miles
away his nearest relative

Walking. *Enclosed are prearrangement*
funeral contracts for Muriel and me.
Also copy of my living Will
and Durable Power of Attorney. With
love to you and the family.

P.S. My date of birth is August 4, 1913.

I should bury him and his sister
back here he wants. Let him want. Let him
tell me why and he was there

I buried two years ago born January 24,
1970 my daughter. Let him first tell me
he's sick I know but so?

HOURS OF COLLECTION

Love succeeds
anger so

Nimbly arriving
as to keep
Silence in the court

Past lights out
but well before dawn
at the foot of the cross

Street a gray
shorthaired tabby
garbage truck purring
in a squat on all fours

Before stealing
in to collect

HOME FOR THE HOLIDAY

Christmas in Pennsylvania
Station he sought the spirit
two years past of the moment

he suspected knowledge of his
daughter's sudden death. On a lower
level there he filled the plot

before the final train commanded
to reach Emergency upstate, beneath the pillar
muted glare his map a shard of coffee'd office

scrap bearing witness with the numbers
punched that morning half way
home past frantic summons from his wife.

Now in the morning rush he waited
till the prior occupant let go
the rope, pressing relayed psalms

of ice over every searing train
pronouncement, deftly cuddling
as if about to dust it fine

for prints, the receiver off its manger
and slipped between those un-
forgiving lips a silver wafer.

When he felt the ersatz breath of death
denied, he yanked the cord
kicking in the trap door on which

he stood surrounded by the surging
crowd and watched the instrument
teeter, dangle, sway, curl.

_____

RESERVATION AT "21"

I met the Messiah today
For lunch. Before me
She arrived. When
She rose we kissed then sat

An hour or more
In a haze of mauve
Low ceiling room resembling
"21" before.

Her fluffy-shoulders lilac dress I recognized.
Her auburn waves dove about the same. Though
She wore no pearls at first I came to see
Her eighteenth birthday

Strand appear. At length
She raised my hand to view
Her ring, anointing with a fingertip
Its onyx face now three years past

Her date. We talked of family first, of course;
Her friends. At dessert
She said it wise were
She to leave before me. Would we

Dine again, I asked
And prayed, distracted just
A fraction by the check. When I looked up
The staff was there.

IV

SMALL COMMUTER TO PORTLAND, MAINE

Banking at 15 thousand
feet first
flight for
business solo
since daughter's

death sudden
two years before,
wing seated roughly
his height distant
from throwback silver

bullet headed
spinner's
propeller
pureeing
tannish clods

of coastal soup,
in warm worn
knickers rolling
in reverse
to LaGuardia's infant

name state
North Shore Field
aloft
aboard age five
lime scooter.

HOT DOG

The only dead child
of any one we knew
as kids was Rossen

the kosher deli owner's
son. When he came
home from the war

that way Rossen
pasted a big gold
star in his window

between the hot
dog grill and cash
register. When you

looked in and caught
the angle you saw
Rossen bent

over his machine
zinging pastrami
slices wearing

a dancing gold
star his son gave
him. I saw that star over

50 years ago
the other day at my
daughter's grave.

JESUS MATINEES

Half past two Wednesdays Catholics
—a fair number—would rise up
in silence when their special

buzzer jolted our Queens
classroom, summons a good
hour before our scheduled

parole to their midweek Saint
Teresa's spiritual sparkle, a canny
swap of Byrd's tale of his *schlep*

over the Antarctic or Vasco de Gama's
spice routes for Jesus matinees.
As if aged or made wiser by this in-

cantation, they moved off with short
grainy strokes, an etiquette faith
associates with a seasoned squad

of pallbearers primed to meet
the threat of church front steep
slippery stairs, death's dance

swift bitsy two-step sole
shuffle spilling soft sand-
paper sounds on gathered grievers

below, cargo remaining aloft,
upright. "Early dismissal
for religious instruction,"

they called it. I envied them
their discharge before our
time and think of them now

in the wake of abrupt dismissal,
return tomorrow a fool's
gold dream, of my daughter, 24.

A WAKE NIGHT

Dead in waking life in sleep
   they rise
      in right inside the castle

Polo Grounds
   decades past the old cathedral's
      demolition.

Here he's 40, peak age
   for taking me to games on
      wooden seats three

Wars ago with skipper Ott in
   right below checked off against
      dime scorecards.

She's 20, four years before
   the aneurysm.
      Now it fades

To Shea repeating life
   with me that day
      when HoJo's backwards

Slash to upper deck
   behind the dish pinballs
      off nearby vacant

Plastic seats and
   clung clungs
      dead to her.

Reappearing now replacing
   me he hears
      Grandpa! Wait till

Dad sees this! He says he
   never got one.
      Smile bleached a city street

Filthy melting snow mound
   black needle-
      point grey

He gives her a good swift
   hug. *Sara? Remember?*
      Hon, he died.

For Michael Bugeja

AN OLD TIME WESTERN ROUNDUP

Halloween night you loaded up
the foot of the seamed nylon copped
from your mother's soiled pile with her flour

and saddled up with a crony posse swinging
their own raw puddings along a cold blue
collar Queens cement trail hunting kike

kids to threaten and corner
candy store plate
windows to pound. Today you see that weapon

stands for time. Inside the knot atop
the lump that screams from toe through arch
is where it choked two years ago

the day they called to say all
of a sudden at work
your child fell

at 24. The endless rest on up
and through the hole are nights
that feed on strangled air.

FROM OUR EXHUMED RECORDS:
THE CASE OF MORNING COFFEE

Three times a week before your morning coffee,
   across the Creek a summer sunrise
   visit to a designated Jewish
      slaughterhouse in Williamsburg
      to fetch from freshly cancelled kosher
      calves no more than three days old, this season's

Cancer voodoo for the desperate goes, their life preserving
   livers, beside you bundled neat in butcher brown
   chauffeured home to Queens, where in lieu of
      merely ordinary morning coffee for the patient,
      the stern Norwegian practical nurse, fond of quoting Cold
      War weary Walter Lippmann in the waning morning *Herald Trib,*

Deposits in her charge curled in fetal reverse
   the first of today's black coffee
   enemas, when mated with
      a generous tumbler of juice
      cranked by nurse's hand underneath
      her gutteral utters from the precious livers, might,

The youngish *Mittel-europa* émigré renegade doctor's shattered
   English suggests, arrest and, as well, perhaps, kill
   off the goings-on inside your youngish freshly
      widowed mother. Toward Labor Day,
      however, as the patient has shrunk some more,
      you race to board a newer whisper, bound for an illegal miracle

Elixir, in its vial heart the liquefied leavings of pulverized
    Central American apricot pits, replanted inside
    your mother behind the back
        of her chart by the godly
        Flushing hospital rogue physician.

    Approaching Halloween he stops the fruit.

Smiling, comatose, a little
    girl again, playing
    on a broken
        murmur a duet reprising Great War summer cherry picking
        with an elder brother, she has seen, somehow, to signal, through
the gift
        of a record dropped by her oldest friend, happy 24, just your
daughter's age at death.

JONATHAN EDWARDS PREACHES
TO THE SEA LIONS

On their mansion's burnished ruby
study wall in '59 at 22
he chanced to strike an oil
of her blondish ghost, sister
of an army friend, his host, dis-
charged to Main Line wealth
so great
they raised on their endless estate,
mind you, *seals,* that ate
obsessively.

Once, between Kentucky
basic training M1 rifle practice
lock-and-loads, his friend, in part
of frugal famous Puritan religious
cloth descent, confided in that
80-dollar weekly average paycheck
year his yearly yield
from trusts alone surpassed 200
thousand.

But here
on the wall
she was dead,

fluked
away at 26
by sloppy
anesthesiology.

So what good was all
the recompense of seals?

Still,
last night at 59
he pricked his nightly skin-
tight ghost, imagining,

though fact,
this time the two years'
gone at 24 sister of his son
starring in that tipped old
gold frame, and he without
a bracing seal to feed.

SUCCEEDING MR. GREEN

Before, standing,
behind the counter
behind the window
of his tiny Cigar
& Candy on the edge of the pie slice awaiting
Queens Boulevard at Greenpoint Avenue,

then, bent,
when he went,
my friend of a friend
Albert Green's widower father,

after Albert traveling to a Jersey ski weekend
at 24 was electrocuted owing to storm downed wires
fallen there when he went for the luggage rack.

Horrified
but fascinated
told a day out of the Army,
I occasionally would make the five
or six blocks then gun past that window
downing quick shots of the tasteless chilling liquor in

the look
of a father
gypped suddenly

of child. Before today I could resurrect
just one child of a father dead
young, until I saw not
three years past my daughter's surprise

end at 24, a man asking how I felt appeared to put
the question from the street side of that window
with the panatelas painted on.

REFLECTING POOL IN WINTER

Alone in the cold on his knees with a dime
and raw palms he dug and brushed away the ginger
earth that covered the top and filled
the holes that made the thing look so old

Through the top of the box on my back
I squint against an early autumn sun
although, of course, if technically,
the top is such thick pine. From deep
within our New Year's dark I face

But pebbles remained embedded. By the time
he stopped so had his screams. He walked the hundred
yards or so to where they keep the records.
There he asked how best to free the insides.

My father, stopping, pacing, appearing
after an age to retreat, reappearing to intercept
his own occasional scream boomeranging back, unable—
disabled?—to leave until—who can see?

Advised to try a point he used this one
to scoop his daughter's name and date and those
behind and told himself next time to open
a box with a toothbrush with hard bristles.

Raising my knees to the bottom
of the top, kindling, so, the wood
to keep him warm between his
shouts, wondering when and where
he'll stop, and why, imagining, never.

AT FIRST

At first I counted the days
one by one
a week arrived
then the days
the weeks one by one
at the same time
a month arrived
then days weeks months
at the same time
one by one
days by the hundred arrived
then the months by the dozen
one by one the years
one by one—
my daughter
died you see
my first
child
my baby
the rest of my life.

THE COMING OF THE SECOND

Then, you got a late delivery.
In that age he left at four
or five what missed the noon's.
The morning's meant more
of the monthly misery

of bills. Its *baaa* was all grownup. Strays wandered
into your lobby row box at four
or five, the last lamb, lazing: a *STAMPS*
magazine, say; or better: its delicious issue: more
send-away-for penny-and-up "approvals" you squandered

allowance quarters on philatelically.
These scarcer drops at four
or five packed the magic to infatuate well before
you ever met; not knowing the next but hoping for more
of the enchanting unsame you barely could see

teasing through the tiny
snout of the midget cell; those four
or five airholes circling, inviting light
enough, just, to tweak your insides guess. More
God knows than I why

I imagined fate's unfull grown envelope divining
    in reverse
today inside that unmapped continent of four
or five, three years past
the insane moment: more
most magic second mail dropped to abrogate
    our daughter's hearse:

a soft bond bed of scripture black-on-cream
identical at first to its four
or five line ancestor: *The family of Sara Bennett*
rescinds with joy its late acknowledgment of sympathy.
    —O is there ever more!
Our death we wish to stress is now
    a dream.

Acknowledgements
(Zei gezunt, fir un tsvantsik!)

Susan Mishler   Michael Bugeja   Roslyn Marcus

Mark Duffy   Robin Martin Parker   Lisa Jackowski

Jo-Ann Ionnotti   Kristen Sassano   Tiffany Weston   Don McKay

Antoinette Bosco   Lois Darby   John Bramblett

Jill Peláez Baumgaertner   Poets House   William Maxwell

Davyne Verstandig   Dave Johnson   Nancy Shear

Jennifer Bosveld   Annette Kramer   Anita Garland

Ric Bollinger   John Taylor-Convery

About the Author

Saul Bennett grew up in the Borough of Queens in New York City and attended Stuyvesant High School in Manhattan before enrolling at Ohio University for journalism. He became a newspaper reporter, then settled into the world of business, occupying him for many years, culminating in his appointment as president of a Madison Avenue public relations group. His articles have appeared in national publications; his poems, in a variety of journals. *New Fields and Other Stones* is his first collection of poems.

Publisher's Dedication

With the kind permission of the author, the publisher further dedicates this book to Kevin, Wendy and Kari Watson—three more who are gone too soon.

This first English language edition of *New Fields and Other Stones*
was printed for Archer Books by Cushing-Malloy in August 1998.
Typeface is Minion Condensed, a 1990 Adobe Originals typeface
by Robert Stimbach, inspired by the classical, old style typefaces
of the late Renaissance, a period of elegant, beautiful and highly
readable type designs. Designed, composed and set by John Taylor-
Convery. Produced by Rosemary Tribulato.